penduka

STUDY GUIDE
& JOURNAL

JOY MCMILLAN

CONTENTS

PENDUKA
prayer

Good morning, God.
Thank you for breathing life into me today.
Give me eyes to see what you are doing
behind the scenes and beneath the surface.
Help me to trust your heart when I cannot see your hand.
To embrace not only the promise but the process.
To cling to you in the pleasant moments, and in the pain.
There is purpose and redemption for it all.
I choose to be led by faith today, rather than driven by fear.
I will stand on what you say about me over everything else.
Tune my heart to hear your voice and to recognize
your invitation to be brave. Then help me to be obedient.
I choose joy in the small everyday moments where
you're weaving something extraordinary from my ordinary.
Stir up Your creativity in me. Pour out Your grace through me.
Help me to exhale the life you have breathed into me.
I am awake. You are good.
Do your thing.

BREATHE IN, BREATHE OUT

PASSION

"I would rather die of passion
than of boredom"

VINCENT VAN GOGH

CHAPTER 1

P | PURSUE JOY

"Joy does not simply happen to us.
We have to choose joy and keep choosing it"

HENRI NOUWEN

Can you recall a time when you were able to endure the pain of a season of your life, though completely devoid of pleasure, because of the passion and purpose that fueled you? From where did you draw your strength and what part did joy play in it?

_____

_____

_____

_____

_____

If joy cannot be stolen, only surrendered, on what altars do you tend to sacrifice your joy and to whom do you tend to give it away?
(ie. over-committed schedule, financial strain, demanding parents/boss/husband, etc.)

_____

_____

_____

In what way will you seek to cultivate more joy in your life today? List 3
simple things (actions, choices, thought/perspective changes, etc.):

_____

_____

_____

How might you better protect your joy reserves from the things/people who
threaten to swallow them whole?

_____

_____

_____

In what simple way could you spread joy today?

_____

_____

DOODLES & TAKEAWAYS

CHAPTER 2

A | ASK QUESTIONS

"Before I can tell my life what I want to do with it,
I must listen to my life telling me who I am"

PARKER PALMER

What were your favorite things to do as a child? _____

_____

What makes your heart happy now? (projects, activities, hobbies, etc.)

_____

_____

What do you get completely engrossed in, that you lose track of time?

_____

_____

What do you love to do, despite the cost or sacrifice it requires?

_____

What moves you deeply? (anger over injustice, joy over convictions, etc.)

_____

_____

What part of what you do now would you do for free? _____

What do you have a knack for that others struggle with? (skills, talents, etc.)

What do you find people come to you for help with? _____

Who do you admire, and what inspires you most about them? (leaders,

teachers, artists, etc.) _____

If you were unexpectedly handed a microphone and asked to teach for 10

minutes, what would you speak about? _____

If you were given free credit at a local university, what classes would you

take? _____

What activity, when you're doing it, makes your spirit come alive? _____

What hardship have you endured in your life that you now find yourself led

to encourage others through? _____

_____

_____

_____

What irks you? Sometimes we're 'anointed for what annoys us' (to be the

solution to the problem we're criticizing): _____

_____

What would you do if you weren't the least bit afraid? _____

_____

_____

Can you spot the common thread stitched through your answers, and

throughout your life? What single sentence sums it up? _____

_____

_____

Grab onto this thread and follow it, it's going to lead you places, girlfriend!

DOODLES & TAKEAWAYS

CHAPTER 3

S | SILENCE COMPARISON

"We won't be distracted by comparison
If we're captivated with purpose"

BOB GOFF

Describe a time when you felt 'threatened' by another woman's creative expression? What was at the root of your response? (i.e. fear, inadequacy, jealousy). How did you feel about yourself in that moment?

_____

_____

_____

How might taking your eyes off others and keeping focused on your lane bring greater freedom and energy to what you're doing (or longing to do)?

_____

_____

How will you keep this at the forefront of your mind next time the temptation to compare flares up?

_____

_____

With a broader understanding of creativity, what creative expression do you enjoy the most? How often do you get to express it?

_____

_____

In what way does your 'offering' add beauty to the world and meet a need? Don't shrug and assume it doesn't. It's in you for a reason, and there's a life-changingly beautiful answer to this one if you're willing to sit with it long enough to really find out.

DOODLES & TAKEAWAYS

CHAPTER 4

S | SURROUND YOURSELF

*"Call it a clan, call it a network, call it a tribe,
call it a family. Whatever you call it,
whoever you are, you need one."*

JANE HOWARD

Who are the five people in your inner circle, and how does each of them influence your emotional and physical health, your spiritual growth, and your vocational endeavors?

_____

_____

_____

_____

_____

_____

_____

_____

_____

_____

Where do you need to establish firmer boundaries in your relationships?

_____

_____

_____

_____

When do you intend to start implementing these? _____

Where are you feeling the ache of isolation or loneliness the most?
In what way can you reach out and bravely step into - or spearhead -
a tribe of women who will meet this need for community in your life?

_____

_____

_____

_____

DOODLES & TAKEAWAYS

CHAPTER 5

I | INSPECT YOUR ROOTS

"Confidence on the outside begins by living
with integrity on the inside."

BRIAN TRACY

Where have you tended to place the most value; on what you see *above* the surface, or what grows *beneath*? Where is this most evident? (relationships, beauty, business image, religious practice, etc.)

_____

_____

_____

_____

_____

How has the inspection of others' (external) fruit taken your focus off of your own (internal) root system's health?

_____

_____

_____

_____

Where do you need to get your hands dirty this week? _____

_____

_____

_____

_____

How can you nurture and tend to your roots today? _____

_____

_____

DOODLES & TAKEAWAYS

CHAPTER 6

O | OWN YOUR STORY

"Owning our story can be hard, but not nearly as
difficult as spending our lives running from it."

BRENE BROWN

Is there a chapter of your story you've been avoiding? What are the major
emotions that arise when you 'go there'?

_____

_____

_____

_____

Where can you identify fear and shame as driving forces behind your
tendency to hide? What is it you're really hiding? Journal some raw, messy
thoughts...

_____

_____

_____

_____

_____

_____

Who can you enlist to come alongside you as you sit with these emotions, process through the pain, and search for the treasure in the dirt?

We empower the voice we choose to listen to - hope or fear, life or death, redemption or shame - how do you plan to silence the negative chatter that holds you captive, and cling to the grace-laced destiny that calls you into the light? (examples would be: write life-giving affirmations, bible verses and quotes on index cards for visible reminders, ask friends to hold you accountable, schedule an appointment with a counselor, etc.)

If it's really true that our pain and suffering can serve a purpose and that our stories can encourage others, name three people who might need to hear yours - unrefined and imperfect as the telling may be.

DOODLES & TAKEAWAYS

CHAPTER 7

N | NEVER EVER GIVE UP

"Miracles start to happen when you give as much
energy to your dreams as you do to your fears."

RICHARD WILKINS

Part of the passion journey is simply zooming out and honoring the path
you've taken. From this aerial perspective you can mine the treasure from
the twists and turns. If you look back through what may have felt like time
wasted, insignificant work done or frustrating detours travelled, where can
you identify:

...an exposure to new things that tapped into your passion?

...a level of training or equipping for what you're ultimately called to do?

...connections with key people who played a part in making you who you
are today?

With the big picture in mind, where are you able to identify struggles or trials
you've endured that have been redeemed and used to fuel your passion,
and your compassion, rather than hinder them?

_____

_____

_____

Now let's zoom back in. Another key part of tapping into your passion is discovering and honing your authentic voice. This is essentially your unique way of expressing yourself and the way you present yourself to the world, be it through writing, speaking or creating. It's also fleshed out in the way you connect with and serve others in your daily encounters. How would you describe your authentic voice? (fiery, tender, instructive, prescriptive, compassionate, transparent, bold, funny, empathetic, truthy, humble, wise, collaborative, etc.)

_____

_____

_____

_____

DOODLES & TAKEAWAYS

PURPOSE

"The place God calls you to is the place where your deep gladness and the world's deep hunger meet"

FREDERICK BUECHNER

CHAPTER 8

P | POWER UP YOUR STRENGTHS

" Hide not your talents. They for use were made.
What's a sundial in the shade?"

BENJAMIN FRANKLIN

Take a few of the tests and assessments listed in your book and record your results here (it will serve as a great resource to return to when you want to compare your results over time, or revisit your strengths and giftings):

☐ _____

☐ _____

☐ _____

☐ _____

☐ _____

☐ _____

☐ _____

☐ _____

☐ _____

_____

_____

_____

We need outside eyes for clarity and to reflect back to us the things we don't see. Take some time to interview a few of your friends and family with these two questions (as uncomfortable as it may be - don't get shy and dismiss what they have to say): "What would you say makes me *me*?" and "What are my top two strongest qualities, where you feel I naturally shine?"

In areas where you're weaker, who could you come alongside - someone who is strong in these areas - to help fill in these 'gaps' in your life? And whose weak areas could you help fill in (personally or professionally)?

DOODLES & TAKEAWAYS

CHAPTER 9

U | UNEARTH THE PICTURE

"The two most important days in your life are the day
you are born and the day you find out why."

MARK TWAIN

In this chapter we unpacked the idea of living backwards. Take some time to think about your eulogy; what would you want the *central theme* to be? This theme would be poignantly expressed by loved ones and reinforced by those who simply watched you flesh out your passion and purpose from a distance (neighbors, community members, readers, followers, students, clients, etc.).

_____

_____

_____

_____

_____

_____

_____

Mission statements act as a guide, providing direction and focus to the participants. A *personal* mission statement consists of 3 key parts:

1. **What do I want to do?** This flows from your *passion*, and is colored by past experience and core values.

2. **Who do I want to help?** This connects your passion to a *need*. This is the value your life will add to the lives of others.

3. What will be the result? This puts meat on the bones and skin in the game. It's where you'll spell out your *end goal*; the thread you want evident throughout your eulogy.

Hash out each of these 3 pieces individually, then go back through them pulling key words and phrases out to form your mission statement. It doesn't have to flow in that order necessarily, but it should contain all three elements; the action, the who, and the ultimate effect.

1. _____

2. _____

3. _____

For example, mine is: *to encourage, equip and empower women through creative communication, coaching and life-giving design, to live their lives bravely, freely and fully.* This, to me, is the most loving thing I can do!

MY PERSONAL MISSION:

_____

_____

_____

_____

_____

While the wording of your mission may evolve slightly as you revisit and review it over time, it acts as a blueprint for your future and a mirror in the present, keeping you focused on what matters at the end of the day.

Now go and live out – and love out - your purpose with boldness; from your eulogy *backwards*, with your mission *before* you.

CHAPTER 10

R | REDEFINE SUCCESS

"I used to be afraid of failing at something that
really mattered to me, but now I'm more afraid
of succeeding at things that don't matter"

BOB GOFF

How do you tend to define success in your own life?

_____

_____

Recall a time that you accomplished something *big* that you'd worked
tirelessly toward, only to find that achieving it didn't satisfy you the way you
expected it to? What do you feel was missing? What would have changed
the experience for the positive (added value)?

_____

_____

_____

_____

_____

How will a shallow, two-dimensional view of success impact what you're
dreaming up, or working on, today? How will it hinder the process and
diminish the outcome?

_____

_____

_____

_____

What myths do you need to confront and thought patterns do you need to get rid of in order to embrace a more otherly-focused, value-driven view of success from here on out?

_____

_____

_____

_____

_____

DOODLES & TAKEAWAYS

CHAPTER 11

P | PULL THOSE WEEDS

"The only thing that stands in between you
and your dreams is the will to try and
the belief that it is actually possible"

JOEL BROWN

As you've read through this chapter, what is stirring in your heart? What is resonating with you the most, thought-pattern wise?

_____

_____

_____

_____

_____

In which area of your life do you suspect you may have some chains lurking (relationally in your marriage or friendships, creatively in your hobbies or vocation, physically in the way you view your body, etc.)?

_____

_____

_____

_____

_____

Who could come alongside you (a spouse, best friend, mentor, etc.) to help you process through your limiting beliefs? Might professional help be a wise move?

_____

_____

_____

When do you plan to reach out to them? _____

DOODLES & TAKEAWAYS

CHAPTER 12

O | OVERFLOW THE INPUT

"Getting the most out of life isn't about how much you
keep for yourself but how much you pour into others"

DAVID STODDARD

Think back to a time when the counsel and wisdom of another influenced
your decisions and in doing so, impacted the course of your life.

_____

_____

_____

_____

If you haven't already done so, write a quick note of thanks to that
person and let them know how valuable their input was.

For the specific season you're in now, is there someone who comes to mind
that you could reach out to and come alongside to learn from and glean
wisdom from?

_____

_____

_____

_____

When and how do you plan to muster the courage to reach out?
Be specific and check it off once you have.

Date: _____ ☐

With the passion and experience you have right now, who could you step back and link arms with for a season? Are there a couple of young women who come to mind who might benefit from the insight and encouragement you could offer them? How could you better position yourself to be available and approachable to them?

_____

_____

_____

_____

_____

_____

DOODLES & TAKEAWAYS

CHAPTER 13

S | STUDENT STATUS

"A teachable spirit is being willing to be a student in any areas you lack, to seek out knowledge and truth, in order to grow in humility, wisdom and excellence."

HOLLY NOEL

What is one big audacious thing that's been stirring in your heart for some time now? (learning a new language, finally writing that book, starting a business, etc.)

_____

_____

_____

What is one thing you could do each day to 'eat the elephant'?

[] _____

What would you be willing to give up in order to make it happen (which requires that you ask yourself, "How badly do I want this?")?

[] _____

[] _____

[] _____

What would it cost for you to wholeheartedly follow the dreams in your heart (I'm not talking exclusively about financial cost)? Would it be worth it in the end? What are you going to do about it?

_____

_____

_____

_____

_____

What are your top 3 time suckers in your day/week/month?

[ ] _____ | _____

[ ] _____ | _____

[ ] _____ | _____

In what simple way could you add learning and growing to your schedule each day? How do you plan to do it and when?

_____

How: _____   When: _____

DOODLES & TAKEAWAYS

CHAPTER 14

E | EMBRACE FAILURE

"There is no comparison between that which is lost by
not succeeding and that which is lost by not trying"

FRANCIS BACON

How do you tend to define failure in your own life?

_____

_____

Think back to a time that you failed stunningly. And I mean *totally bombed*
at something. What happened?

_____

_____

_____

What are 3 positive things you took away from that experience or learned
about yourself in the process?

1. _____

2. _____

3. _____

As you look ahead, where do you fear failure the most?

_____

_____

_____

Unpack why it strikes fear into your heart the way it does, and find the underlying statement. What belief is behind that fear? And how valid is that?

_____

_____

_____

_____

In what simple way can you practice bravery this week? How can you get out of your comfort zone and take a risk? Record when you plan to do it, and then come back and jot down how it went in the 'Doodles & Takeaways' section below once you've stepped out.

What? _____

When? _____

DOODLES & TAKEAWAYS

PROCESS

"It is not enough to be busy;
so are the ants. The questions is:
What are we busy about?"

HENRY DAVID THOREAU

CHAPTER 15

P | PROTECT YOUR YES

*"Learn to say "no" to the good
so you can say "yes" to the best."*

JOHN C. MAXWELL

Be still for a moment and take your soul's pulse. Are you weary and running on empty? How does your schedule look? What have you given your yes to that you know you should have said *no* to?

_____

_____

_____

_____

_____

When you've honored your commitment and seen these things through, how do you plan to excuse yourself from them in the future? Having your solid 'no' prepared will help you deliver it even under pressure.

_____

_____

_____

What have you said *no* to in the past that you know you need to say yes to today?

_____

_____

Who (spouse, children, yourself, God, etc.) have you inadvertently said no to by saying yes to other less important things?

_____   _____

_____   _____

In what way can you communicate to them this week that you choose them?

_____

_____

What will you have to say no to in order to make this happen?

_____   _____

_____   _____

What small but significant thing can you say NO to today?

_____

What small but significant thing can you say YES to today?

_____

DOODLES & TAKEAWAYS

CHAPTER 16

R | REPEAT IT & REAP

*"If you always do what you've always done,
you'll always get what you've always got."*

HENRY FORD

What simple practice could you start doing today, and commit to for the next 30 days, for which your future self would thank you?

_____

What areas of your life do you struggle the most to apply consistency and good habits?

_____   _____

_____   _____

_____   _____

What single, small daily habit could you implement in each area to start reshaping your day? When do you plan to start?

_____   _____

_____   _____

_____   _____

Starting: _____

What small bad habits could you remove from your daily life that would reap a big reward over time?

_____

- [ ] _____
- [ ] _____
- [ ] _____
- [ ] _____

DOODLES & TAKEAWAYS

CHAPTER 17

O | OPEN UP SPACE

"When a man is wrapped up in himself,
he makes a pretty small package."

J O H N   R U S K I N

The by-product of a life without margin is stress and overwhelm. Where are
you feeling a lack of margin the most?

_____

_____

_____

_____

What can you do, moving forward, to carve out more white space in the
different areas of your life?

_____

_____

What do you feel is the appeal of internet friendships? Where might there
be a lack of transparency or authenticity creeping into your life?

_____

_____

As you've worked your way through what might be the hardest chapter to
swallow, who comes to mind in regard to your local community and
neighborhood?

_____

_____

_____

_____

_____

Who could you reach out to *this week* to initiate a friendship or take the next step to deepening an existing one?

⬚ _____   ⬚⬚ _____

⬚ _____   ⬚⬚ _____

Decide on a night of the week, once a month (you decide the 'schedule') and commit to inviting a new family, couple or single person over for dinner. It doesn't have to be fancy - *connection* is what matters. Write out a few names that come to mind in the space below, then jot down when and how you plan on reaching out to them:

DOODLES & TAKEAWAYS

CHAPTER 18

C | CRASH THE COMPARTMENTS

"We ought not to attempt to cure the eyes without
the head, or the head without the body...
the body without the soul. For the part can
never be well unless the whole is well."

PLATO

Use the space on the right to jot down your responses:

PHYSICAL:

• How is my health on a scale of 1 to 10?
10 being energetic and vibrantly healthy.

• How am I fueling my body? Is what I'm
putting in it nourishing and nurturing it or
slowly destroying it?

• Am I moving more than I'm sitting? Am I
making use of this beautiful body I've been
given, or am I assuming it will continue to
function well without maintenance or care?

• Am I eating as colorfully and freshly as
possible, or does my diet consist of various
shades of pre-packaged browns?

• Am I aware of when I'm satisfied,
or do I frequently eat until I'm
uncomfortably stuffed?

• Do I take the time to care for myself daily,
doing whatever little things make me feel
pretty and lovely (perfume, make-up,
earrings, etc.)?

- Do I consistently get enough sleep? Do I take time to rest and be still?

- Do I consistently take a multivitamin?

- Am I hydrating my body sufficiently with clean, unadulterated water?

- Based on the number I selected in the first question, what is one thing I can do today to take my physical health up to the next number?

MENTAL & EMOTIONAL:

- How do I feel on a scale of 1 to 10? 10 being hopeful and excited about my future.

- How intentional am I at cultivating an attitude of gratitude?

- Am I truly aware of my intrinsic worth and value or am I allowing others to determine or diminish it?

- Am I resilient? Do I bounce back quickly or do I obsess over failure and hurt feelings?

- Am I communicating my needs and boundaries or am I expecting others to guess correctly and meet them?

- Do I regularly choose peace over being right?

- Am I intentionally nourishing and expanding my mind, or do I consume soul-sucking junk on a regular basis?

- Am I carving out time to do things that make me come alive and fuel my soul?

• Am I over-committed and stretched-thin or am I mastering the art of saying "no"?

• Based on the number I selected in the first question, what is one thing I can do today to take my emotional health up to the next number?

SPIRITUAL:

• How's my relationship with God on a scale of 1 to 10? 10 being authentic, intimate and growing.

• Am I feeding my spirit more than I feed my flesh (in what I read, watch and listen to)?

• How's my 'fruit'; joy, peace, patience, kindness, self-control, etc.?

• Is my relationship with God a one-way street, or am I being still long enough to hear His heart?

• Am I looking for simple ways to daily impact other people's eternity, even if just by loving them well?

• Am I inward focused and self-absorbed or do I look for opportunities to bless and serve others?

• Do I look for God's fingerprints in hard times or do I tend to assume He's punishing me?

• Do I fall into the trap from going through religious motions or am I working to cultivate authentic spirituality and intimacy with God?

• Am I generous with my resources, out of my understanding of His sufficiency, or do I struggle with a poverty mentality?

• Based on the number I selected in the first question, what is one thing I can do today invest in my spiritual life and bump it up a number?

The results of this evaluation are intended to bring awareness in these three dimensions of your life (physical, mental/emotional & spiritual).

Now ask yourself what you can do today...tomorrow, this week...that will have a positive impact on your physical health, your emotional and mental health, and your personal walk with God?

_____

_____

_____

_____

_____

_____

Where do you want to be a year from now?

_____

_____

_____

_____

_____

What do you want to see changed first? And what baby steps can you take toward making this happen?

DOODLES & TAKEAWAYS

CHAPTER 19

E | EXIT HERE, PERFECTION

"The thing that is really hard, and really amazing,
is giving up on being perfect and beginning
the work of becoming yourself."

ANNA QUINDLEN

Where do you see perfectionism showing up most clearly in your life?

Jot down an area or two and then ask yourself a series of "what" and "why"
questions until you uncover the root of your pursuit, recording your questions
and answers.

For example: Why do I feel as though perfection in my looks is the only
acceptable option? What or who has led me to believe that my value is
connected to the way I look? Okay, if I don't *truly* believe that my worth is
directly connected to others' ability to acknowledge me as pretty or slim or
attractive, why would I allow that concern to continue to steal my joy? Why
would I risk communicating to my daughter that her outward appearance
has anything to do with our inner worth by feeding the lie myself? What
would help me embrace and celebrate my unique beauty on a daily basis?

Keep going until you feel you've found the underlying issue and dealt with it
at the root level (use the Doodles & Takeaways section if you want to map it
out). Don't hesitate to enlist the help of a professional if you discover these
roots are deeper and more entangled than you anticipated.

If you *don't* struggle with perfectionism, where do you tend to hold the bar especially high? If this has been a trend, might it be time to reevaluate the placement of that bar?

What is one thing you plan to put into action this week - regardless of whether you're excited about it as yet or whether it's perfectly presentable - with the sole intention of getting the ball rolling and momentum building?

DOODLES & TAKEAWAYS

CHAPTER 20

S | STOP SWITCHTASKING

"Concentrate all your thoughts upon the work at hand.
The sun's rays do not burn until brought to a focus."

ALEXANDER GRAHAM BELL

When are you most tempted to 'multitask'? What do you believe drives the
temptation in this area? (boredom, creative avoidance, habit, etc.)

_____

_____

_____

What would this period of your day look like if you chose to focus on only
one thing at a time? (map it out)

MY ONE THING

If you're prone to checking your phone often, be it work or the mindless scroll that keeps you there, who in your inner circle feels the weight of this the most? How will this habit impact this relationship in the long run? What are you going to do about it?

_____

_____

_____

Now that you understand the reality of switchtasking, and what it does to your ability to focus and produce results, map out your ideal week below, cutting each day into chunks or blocks - assigning a single focus to each time period. Commit to trying this for just three weeks, tweaking and reevaluating as you go, and see if it transforms your ability to stay engaged and get what matters done.

MY IDEAL WEEK

CHAPTER 21

S | START SMALL

"Do not despise these small beginnings,
for the Lord rejoices to see the work begin..."

ZECHARIAH 4:10

How do you focus on and celebrate the small things? If you don't, what simple practice could you add to your day to aid in reflecting on and celebrating the small wins (even if just for a season)?

_____

_____

_____

When do you plan to start? _____

As numerous studies recorded in the Harvard Business Review revealed, small wins matter greatly. People who won the lottery were far less happy over time compared to people who had simple routines in place that boosted their spirits, like attending a weekly church service. Obviously, big isn't always better.

If our small everyday moments influence our lives far more than the epic ones we typically strive for, what 3 simple habits or connection points could you implement into your week that would help nurture passion and line up with your greater purpose (physical health, spiritual growth, deeper social connection, etc.)

_____

_____

_____

_____

With the process and expectation gap in mind, what do you find to be the hardest part of being en route? Where are you in the journey and what can you take with you to keep you focused and encouraged to the end?

DOODLES & TAKEAWAYS

"Don't ask what the
world needs.
Ask what makes you
come alive, and go do it.
Because what the
world needs
is people who
have come alive."

HOWARD THURMAN

NOTES

DOODLES

NOTES

DOODLES

NOTES

DOODLES

NOTES

The Voyage

Speak, even if your voice is trembling
Please, you've been quiet for so long
Believe it'll be worth the risk you're taking

You're afraid,
But you can hear adventure calling
There's a rush of adrenaline to your bones
What you make of this moment changes everything

What if the path you choose becomes a road
What if the path you take becomes your home
The wind is high, but the pressure's off
I'll send the rain wherever we end up
Wherever we end up

Set your sights
Set them far beyond the familiar
In the rising tides
You find the rhythm of your heart
Lift your head
Now the wind and waves don't matter

The path you choose becomes a road
The ground you take becomes your home
The wind is high, but the pressure's off
I'll send the rain wherever we end up
Wherever we end up

I am the wind in your sails

AMANDA COOK | BRAVE NEW WORLD

FIND OUT MORE ABOUT

penduka

SHOP THE PENDUKA STORE:

PENDUKALIFE.ORG/STORE

Have questions or a story to tell?
Share thoughts about your Penduka journey at:

PENDUKALIFE.ORG/CONTACT

stay tuned for the

PENDUKA PODCAST | FALL 2016

#PENDUKALIFE

CONNECT WITH JOY

facebook.com/simplybloom
Instagram.com/simplybloomjoy
joy@simplybloom.org

Invite Joy to speak at your next women's event:
SIMPLYBLOOM.ORG/SPEAKING

For more information about coaching & consulting:
SIMPLYBLOOM.ORG/COACHING

LIKE #HAPPYMAIL?

Write a note to Joy and she'll zip a quick note
of encouragement back to you:

Joy McMillan | PO Box 373 | Merrill, MI 48637

ABOUT THE AUTHOR

Joy McMillan is the founder of Simply Bloom
Productions LLC, a creative little company
with a big heart and an even bigger dream.

A writer, speaker, graphic designer, mentor & coach,
she loves helping women embrace their stores, live out
their purpose with passion, and leave legacies of love.

Founder of the #weROARproject and creative
whirlwind behind the Simply Bloom shop, she's the author
of XES, The New Author's Launch Manual & Penduka.

Originally hailing from Southern Africa, Joy lives and loves
in Michigan with her hubby and their two little loin-fruit.

SIMPLYBLOOM.ORG

30753057R00045

Made in the USA
Middletown, DE
05 April 2016